I mBÉAL AN BHÁIS

THE GREAT FAMINE AND THE LANGUAGE SHIFT IN NINETEENTH-CENTURY IRELAND

GEARÓID Ó TUATHAIGH

This essay is part of the interdisciplinary series *Famine Folios*,
covering many aspects of the Great Hunger in Ireland from 1845-52.

CONTENTS

Figure 1 | Joseph Patrick Haverty, *The Monster Meeting at Clifden in 1843* [Detail]

INTRODUCTION

The Great Irish Famine of 1845-51 was a subsistence crisis and a social calamity without parallel in nineteenth-century Europe. The failure in successive seasons of a single root crop – the potato – resulted in excess mortality of over one million (from starvation and a range of hunger-related diseases), and precipitated a virtual tidal wave of emigration that would see up to four million flee the country in the twenty years after 1845. Of the approximately 8.5 million population in 1845, it is likely that some three million were almost exclusively dependent on the potato as their survival diet. The failure of the potato – and the utter failure of the government of the most advanced economy in the world at the time to respond adequately to the crisis – resulted in the decimation of the rural underclass. It set in train a chain of continuing emigration that would see the population of Ireland fall from approximately 6.6 million in 1851 to 4.4 million in 1911. It decisively altered the class structure of rural Ireland. Inevitably, it was a drastic agent of social change.

Arguably the most fundamental social and cultural change in modern Irish history was the shift from Irish to English as the vernacular of the population at large. This study examines the role of the Great Famine in this remarkable drama of cultural transformation.

The complex question of whether the Famine – unquestionably the greatest social calamity ever to befall Ireland – was a turning-point or a brutal accelerator of social and economic trends already in train in the pre-Famine decades has been central to the historiography of the Famine for a long time. The demographic aspect is a case in point, where one would imagine that it might be possible to delineate with some precision the impact of the calamity. There are difficulties in so doing, owing to the shortcomings of the 1841 census, and the resulting difficulties in extrapolating population movement during the Famine decade itself, up to the 1851 census.[1] But for all that, we can say that the Famine decimated the rural underclass, turning a rising tide of emigration into a torrent and firmly establishing a pattern that would make emigration a central aspect of Irish social history for well over a century after 1850. The Famine transformed the social structure of Irish rural society, removing hundreds of thousands of the rural poor and hundreds of encumbered landlords, and decisively shifting the balance (social, economic, and cultural) in much of the country in favor of the commercial-farming and urban middle classes. Of course, there were marked regional variations in the pace and thoroughness of this transformation, as the growing number of local studies over the past two decades has demonstrated.

Nonetheless – the many difficulties and challenges relating to the reliability of various data notwithstanding – it is possible to consider the impact of the Famine on the demographic and social structure of Irish society with some degree of assurance, addressing the question whether the calamity was a decisive turning-point or a violent accelerator of existing trends. Indeed, the data of the 1841 and the 1851 censuses have been carefully mined to create an impressive cartographic representation of the main economic and social (including demographic) dimensions of the impact of the Famine.[2]

What has proved more resistant to close quantitative analysis is the impact that the Famine may have had on key domains of the socio-cultural life of the people, their beliefs and rituals, customs, habits, and cultural practices. This is especially the case in relation to the two central aspects of cultural practice in the lives of the common people: their religious culture and their language. The census data, upon which the impact of the Famine on aggregate (and local) demographic change has been estimated, do not facilitate accurate calibration of change (within the crucial decade 1841–51) in cultural practices relating to religion and language-use.[3]

A striking reading of the cultural impact of the Famine, and one that links religious and linguistic aspects of cultural production and practice, was Emmet Larkin's hypothesis that the exceptional Irish conformity to formal Catholic observance and devotion was, in a complex psychological way, a fervent assertion of religious identity as a compensation for the sense of cultural loss caused by the abandonment of the Irish language and its replacement by English as the main vernacular. Levels of religious observance and an intensity of devotion unrivalled in the western Christian world was, in some sense, the substitute identity for a people who had "voluntarily" surrendered their native language (Larkin 648-50).

Larkin's chronology for the origins and dissemination of the "devotional revolution" in Irish Catholic practice has been comprehensively revised by scholars in recent decades. But while his overly schematic and chronologically questionable notion of a devotional revolution taking place in Irish Catholicism in the immediate post-Famine generation may have been revised, there is a fundamental insight into aspects of cultural change pivoting on religion and language that is deserving of closer attention. In order to tease out what may be of value in Larkin's hypothesis, it makes sense to set out some basic data regarding the linguistic circumstances of Ireland in the first half of the nineteenth century, and in particular the position of the Irish language as a vernacular in pre-Famine Ireland.

ESTIMATING THE SHIFT

The 1851 census was the first to include a question on language. However, the question was embedded in a series of sub-sections relating to Education and Literacy, and would remain so until 1881, when it became a separate question in its own right (Ó Gliasáin 1-2). The official census returns from 1851 are included in Table A below (Hindley 19):

TABLE A: IRISH-SPEAKING POPULATION 1851-1901

Census date	Total population	Speakers of Irish only		Total Irish speakers	
		Number	%	Number	%
1841	8,175,124	NOT ENUMERATED		NOT ENUMERATED	
1851	6,552,365	319,602	4.9	1,524,286	23.3
1861	5,798,564	163,275	2.8	1,105,536	19.1
1871	5,412,377	103,562	1.9	817,875	15.1
1881	5,174,836	64,167	1.2	949,932	18.2
1891	4,704,750	38,121	0.8	680,174	14.5
1901	4,458,775	20,953	0.5	641,142	14.4

There was considerable under-reporting on this language question in the early censuses (before 1881), with some estimates putting the under-reporting as high as forty percent. Thus, if we adjust the 1851 figure accordingly, we reach a figure of approximately 2.13 million Irish speakers, with perhaps as many as half a million of these being monoglots. The figures for 1861 and 1871 might, likewise, need adjustment to account for under-reporting. The improved enumeration (and separate question) in 1881 means that those census figures are likely to be closer to the mark. However, we must also allow for social-psychological factors in self-reporting on the language question: prior to 1891, knowledge of English is likely to have been exaggerated, and the figures for monoglot Irish speakers probably underestimated, while in subsequent censuses (as the Gaelic League language revival project began to influence public attitudes) it is possible that the figure for Irish speakers was exaggerated.[4]

Estimates for the number (and percentage) of Irish speakers in the pre-Famine period are simply that – estimates – and they vary widely, from approximately 1.5 to four million. If we allow a figure of close to 2.13 million in 1851 (as suggested above), then it would not be unreasonable to suggest a figure of around three million in 1845, given the heavy Famine mortality among the poorest classes of the rural population and in the western half of the country – the classes and regions with the heaviest concentration of Irish speakers.[5] However, the actual figures, in whatever manner we estimate them, are less important, in the context of the decisive shift in the vernacular, than the data on the pace and direction of the language shift that we can identify in the pre-Famine decades. Here, Fitzgerald's painstaking statistical exercise in working backwards from later censuses (notably those of 1851–81 and 1901), in order to identify the language transmission pattern for cohorts born in successive decades from the 1770s to 1901, provides a more secure statistical basis for delineating (over time and geographically) the pattern of Ireland's language shift. His calculations suggest that only twenty-eight percent of children born in the 1830s grew up with a knowledge of Irish. Moreover, while upwards of forty percent of the population may have been Irish-speaking in 1800, only fifteen percent, perhaps, were monoglot Irish speakers (Fitzgerald, "Estimates for Baronies" and "Irish Speaking").

Most pertinent to our focus here on the impact of the Great Famine, Fitzgerald demonstrated statistically what earlier studies had suggested, that the abandonment of Irish and the shift to English as the main vernacular was accelerating during the opening three decades of the nineteenth century. His conclusions are deserving of extensive quotation:

in the island as a whole [...] in the 1770s probably more than half the younger generation must still have been Irish-speaking [...] and in the following three decades this percentage did not decline by very much, c. 1 percent per decade. [...] [E]ven in 1800 the proportion of the younger generation speaking Irish in the island as a whole must still have been close to 50% [...] It was after 1800 that the language began to decline more rapidly. In the following sixty years, the national percentage of Irish-speaking dropped three to four times faster than in the eighteenth century, viz. by 4 to 5 percent per decade (*Ireland in the World* 19).

The data, therefore, clearly indicate that the shift was already accelerating in the three decades before the founding of the "National" schools in 1831 and certainly before the Famine calamity.

So far as the geographical dimension of this language shift is concerned, the broad picture from the mid-eighteenth century is clear. As Liam de Paor noted, if we look at the age cohort born in 1771–81 we see that Munster and Connacht were quite solidly Irish-speaking, but already there was a blurred frontier zone, running from Donegal Bay to the west shore of the Shannon and on to the Barrow, north of lower Suir, showing a weakening in the transmission of Irish. North Donegal and south Kilkenny were still strongly Irish-speaking. Moreover, a wedge of strong Irish speaking was running from Dundalk Bay through Louth, North Meath, parts of Monaghan, and south Armagh. There were reasonably healthy (up to forty percent) levels in parts of mid-Leinster and in the Sperrins, and smaller pockets here and there in Ulster.

The solidly English-speaking areas ran from the Shannon south-east to Wicklow/Wexford (including north Tipperary) and in the north-east (north Down, south Antrim, North Armagh), together with east Donegal; countrywide, the towns were predominantly English-speaking. But if we look at the cohort born ninety years later (1861–71), we see a huge retreat to the Atlantic *Gaeltacht* areas of Donegal, Galway and Mayo, and west Kerry; north Clare was still strong, but, outside of west Cork and part of the Waterford coast, Irish had retreated to residual enclaves elsewhere in Munster, with isolated pockets left in mid-Ulster.[6]

EXPLAINING THE SHIFT

While the improved statistical evidence enables us to describe with greater precision the rate, and inter-generational and geographical aspects of the vernacular language shift, providing a satisfactory explanation – in socio-linguistic or cultural terms – for what was, by European standards, a remarkable historical event, presents a different set of challenges. Essentially, however, the Irish vernacular shift was a function of the conquest of Ireland in the early modern period. In the medieval period the adoption of "the Irish tongue" by the descendants of the Anglo-Norman settlers was identified – from the fourteenth century – as a sign of their lapsing into degeneracy. Laws were promulgated from time to time (the most notorious being the 1366 Statutes of Kilkenny) aimed at halting and reversing such degeneracy. However, with the conquest of Ireland and its absorption into the Tudor (and later Stuart) British state in the sixteenth and seventeenth centuries, the extension of English (and the displacement of Irish) as the general vernacular was seen as an essential aspect of "making Ireland British." The defeat of the Gaelic chieftains and the dissolution of the legal, social, political, and military system on which Gaelic Ireland rested, and the extension of the jurisdiction (and, in time, administrative apparatus) of the crown, shifted the balance of power decisively.[7]

The flight of the Gaelic chieftains at the start of the seventeenth century – with their military and intellectual elites – and the immigration of sizable numbers (by plantation to confiscated land or assisted voluntary migration) throughout the seventeenth century further strengthened the sway of English. Consequently, "English was firmly established as the language of the elite by the beginning of the seventeenth century," and "by the fourth decade of the seventeenth century the tide in the ongoing linguistic ebb and flow between Irish and English in Ireland was flowing strongly in favour of the latter" (Kelly and MacMurchaidh 21 and 15). The dominance of English spread from the east to the west and from the towns to the countryside.

The religious dimension of the Conquest (from the Reformation to the end of the seventeenth century) was intertwined, in complex ways, with the language question.

But, in terms of the conquest, confiscation, and colonization that marked the protracted struggle to render Ireland "safe" within the expanding British state and empire of the early modern period, it was religious loyalty, rather than language, that determined the winners and losers in the game. The defeat and dispossession of the Catholic leadership, and the general Penal Code enacted (after the triumph of William of Orange and the Protestant cause in 1691) to keep Catholics excluded from the political and civic life of the country, left Irish Catholics with a strong shared sense of historical grievance. Gaelic poets might join language with religion as the twin markers of the identity of the defeated people, and see revival or restoration of Catholic fortunes under the Stuarts as a harbinger of the restoration of respect for the Irish language and for its scribes and scholars. But, in truth, a Catholic "revival" from the early seventeenth century onwards did not necessarily, nor did it in fact, mean a restoration of dominant status to the Irish language. [8] An emerging Catholic middle class was prominent in trade and commerce by the mid-eighteenth century, with English as its vernacular.

As the relaxation of the Penal Laws gradually permitted the re-emergence of Catholics into civic life (including the law, education, property ownership and limited political participation) from the final third of the eighteenth century, it was abundantly clear that the advancing and improving elements of the Catholic

Figure 2 | Joseph Patrick Haverty, *The Monster Meeting at Clifden in 1843*

Political mobilization of the ordinary people in the pre-Famine decades by Daniel O'Connell, including large public meetings, was overwhelmingly conducted through English.

community had adopted English as their vernacular. Gaelic poets might lament
the abandonment of Irish by the rising Catholic bourgeoisie, but the evidence was
incontrovertible that, while a Stuart restoration might well bring relief to Irish
Catholics and a measure of patronage to old Gaelic families that had formerly
supported the scribes and poets, a major reversal of the language shift to English was
not a realistic prospect of any Jacobite revival by the early eighteenth century. [9]

RETURNING FROM MARKET, A SCENE IN THE COUNTY OF KILKENNY.—DRAWN BY E. FITZPATRICK.

THE IRISH SCHOOLMASTER.

AMONGST the variety of "professors" that practise on the Irish peasantry in the shape of horse and cow doctors, bone-setters, and fairy men, perhaps there is not a more distinguished individual than the Hedge Schoolmaster.

Educated in a seminary similar to that in which he presides, having there acquired all his former preceptor's knowledge, he has either stepped into his shoes on his demise, or set up an establishment on his own account, trusting his success to the favourable opinion the neighbours had formed of his abilities during his years of probation. The Hedge Schoolmaster is, therefore, greatly respected by the peasantry whose children he has undertaken to educate; he is ever a welcome guest at their homes, gets the best "bit and sup" and the warmest corner at their firesides. Here he seems as much at home and more at his ease than the hospitable owner of the domicile he has condescended to visit, and whom he repays by astonishing with his intimate knowledge of past events, gleaned generally from antiquated newspapers: he can even tell of things to come, in a style equal, if not superior, to the prophetic pages of *Moore's Almanack*, which popular annual he is seldom or ever known to agree with. He is generally, too, a proficient in music, and on Sunday evenings, in the summer time, gives the boys and girls an opportunity of enjoying themselves on "the green" in a jig or country dance to the sounds of his violin. But as human nature is never perfect, even in the wisest of mankind, there is one failing inseparably allied with the Hedge Schoolmaster—he is a little too fond of "the drop;" his indulgence in which, though it occasionally mars his dignity in some respects, is amply atoned for in others; for, as the spirit of the glass ascends to his head, the pent-up *larning* as quickly escapes from that abode in "words of learned length and thundering sound."

Now there may be, as is often the case, a rival schoolmaster in the adjacent village, and he too, either by accident or design, might be present on one of those festive occasions. The meeting of those worthies is as "Greek to Greek." No two gamecocks could regard each other more fiercely, and the encounter of wits is often as decisive and deadly. Here lies the Hedge Schoolmaster's real danger. If in the opinion of the excited company he is put down in the discussion, even on such a point as the "Irish tutor" puzzled the great Dr. O'Toole, when he asked him the exact position Ballyragget occupied on the globe, his fame is gone. The cry is up through the country, "The master was beat in the 'larnin';" and in a day or two the schoolmaster is literally "abroad," his grove deserted, and his pupils fled to his more witty or accomplished rival.

THE IRISH SCHOOLMASTER.—DRAWN BY E. FITZPATRICK.

As a recent study concludes:

What is apparent is that as Ireland was slowly absorbed during the course of the eighteenth century into an economy whose language was English, into a cultural milieu which deemed English the superior language, into an administrative (including legal) system which conducted itself through English, and into a political world whose discourse was conducted in English, the incentives to acquire English to converse, and to learn to read and to write English to function effectively in an increasingly literate world became compelling (Kelly and MacMurchaidh 32).

Thus, "as the end of the eighteenth century approached, it was manifest that English had replaced Irish as the vernacular of choice over much of the country" (Kelly and MacMurchaidh, 32). The state's role and its reach into the lives of ordinary people increased in the decades following Union (notably from the 1820s) and the launch of mass political participation by O'Connell from the mid-1820s was a powerful engine of more intensive socialization – with English as its medium **[Figures 1 and 2]**. [10]

Accordingly, the evidence is clear that the decisive underlying factors in the language shift were already in play before the establishment by the state of its elementary school system from the 1830s, before O'Connell's mass political movements, and before the advent of the Great Famine. But Liam de Paor's arresting verdict – that "The Gaelic world died from the top down. Its political superstructure was destroyed in the sixteenth century. Its social and cultural superstructure was destroyed in the seventeenth century. Its social fabric was destroyed in the eighteenth century" (168) – demands further examination.

The acquisition of English, in any formal sense, required instruction or schooling of some kind. This had been realized by the British state since the time of the Reformation, and a succession of initiatives from the sixteenth century had made provision for various kinds of elementary schools under the auspices of the Established Church. Apart from those established in the plantation counties (notably in Ulster), these initiatives had limited effect. The majority of Catholics depended for basic education on private fee or "hedge" schools.

While such fee or "hedge" schools, on the available evidence, were generally vectors for the acquisition and advance of English, there was considerable variation, as it seems, in their effectiveness. Some of the schoolmasters were native Irish speakers, some actually used Irish in their teaching. But the majority of the Irish-speaking peasantry were not literate in Irish by the beginning of the eighteenth century. [11] From the later eighteenth century, as the relaxation of the Penal Laws removed restrictions on Catholic education, the spread of a miscellany of private schools of various kinds increased Catholic participation. English was the language of this expanding matrix of schools – some under at least indirect Catholic Church patronage and support, as the Catholic revival gathered momentum in the later eighteenth century, and as the

Figure 3 | E. Fitzpatrick, "The Irish School Master" (*The Illustrated London News*, January 24, 1857)

The schoolmaster – responsive to the wishes of the parents and, after 1831, to the rules of the central state system of elementary education – was a key actor in the language shift in Ireland.

increase in population intensified the need for more schools. [12] As Archbishop Oliver Kelly told the 1825 Commission on Education: "The English Language is the only one taught in the schools for the poor" (qtd. in Mahon xvi) **[Figures 3 and 4]**.

By the early nineteenth century, in the aftermath of the revolutionary scare of the 1790s, and in the optimistic belief that the Union created the opportunity for a new start in inculcating habits and values of order and civility among the mass of the Irish people, the state increased its efforts to assist schemes for establishing elementary schools for the Irish poor. The most notable was the Kildare Place Society's network of state-supported and generally well-run schools (founded 1811), whose formula of secular education with bible reading without comment, after initially being accepted by the Catholic Church leaders, was soon mired in charges of assisting proselytizing and seeking to seduce Catholic youth from their church. With the Whig reforms of the 1830s, a new initiative was launched to establish a national, non-denominational system of elementary education under direct state auspices – through a state-appointed Board of Commissioners. [13]

The arrival of the state elementary or "National" schools from the 1830s (while initially absorbing and rebranding many existing schools) clearly gave a new consistency and, allowing for early indifferent attendance rates, standardization to the relentless drive towards literacy and fluency in English. [14] With their standardized (centralized) curriculum and schoolbooks – and the fact that the clergy were the key managerial cohort for most of the system – the schools became not only the citadels of English, but also the nurseries of those Victorian utilitarian values – notions of good order, hygiene (social and personal), and general respectability in behavior – through which the adoption of English was propagated and prized. The spread of Catholic schools run by religious orders dedicated to the education of the poor (nuns and religious brothers) from the close of the eighteenth century through to the pre-Famine decades further consolidated the drive towards language change, whatever may have been the consciousness of an historically rooted sense of Irish Catholic identity that these schools sought to shape and inculcate. [15]

Figure 4 | E. Fitzpatrick, "The Irish School Master" (*The Illustrated London News*, January 24, 1857) [Detail]

Figure 5 | J. Cochran, *John McHale, Archbishop of Tuam*

John McHale was an exception among the Catholic hierarchy in championing the Irish language, not only for pastoral purposes, but also for general cultural objectives, through his own compositions and translations.

LANGUAGE & RELIGIOUS WORSHIP

Central to any consideration of the complex factors driving the language shift in Ireland must be an assessment of the role of the churches; in particular, the catechetical, pastoral, and devotional role of the Catholic Church, the church of the majority. Writing of the key determinants of literacy, Niall Ó Ciosáin has stated that:

Literacy in a language which is not the language of the state or the language of trade and commerce is rooted in religious usage, and its extent is largely determined by the attitudes and actions of institutional churches. Moreover, since literacy which was devotional in origin was used to read secular texts also, the extent of a reading public for all kinds of texts in non-official languages was also largely determined by the extent of the initial impetus given to it by institutional churches ("Pious miscellanies" 270).

The broader issue is whether the Catholic Church played a passive or a drastic role in the change of vernacular in Ireland.

From the politico-religious convulsions of the Reformation to the final defeat of the Jacobite cause in 1691, the Catholic Church had retained the loyalty of the majority of the Irish people. By the end of the seventeenth century it was the church of the defeated and the dispossessed: its bishops and many of its clergy in exile, its institutional and organizational structures (especially relating to the education and training of priests) virtually destroyed. A network of Irish colleges in Catholic Europe provided the platform for the counter-reformation efforts in Ireland. A cluster of clergy (notably the Franciscans at Louvain) provided not only Irish-language devotional and catechetical literature for the Irish mission, but also the canonical historical texts for a form of Catholic nationalism based on recording the glories of the Gaelic civilization and language and refuting the charges of Gaelic barbarism that featured strongly in the propaganda of the English conquest.[16]

Yet, with the gradual reconstruction of the Catholic Church infrastructure in Ireland, consequent on the easing of the Penal Laws from the middle decades of the eighteenth century, the language of this recovering Catholic Church establishment remained predominantly English. In this, the bishops and priests reflected and fortified the language choice of the Irish Catholic bourgeoisie as a whole. This bald statement conceals complex patterns of language use within the life of the Catholic Church and community. Ciarán MacMurchaidh, in describing the era of dependence on the continental colleges for the supply of Irish priests, has suggested that: "At the heart of this problem lay the incapacity of the institutional church to educate and to properly prepare its clergy for ministry in either a monolingual or a bilingual environment" (163). Protection and transmission of the Catholic faith was the priority for church leadership. The bishops were aware of the increasing use of English; but, while certain of the continental colleges made some effort to ensure that the students (many of them very young) kept up their command of Irish, there was neither coherence nor consistency in language preparation for the Irish mission. MacMurchaidh points out that:

as a growing number of Catholics became bilingual, an increasingly bilingual laity provided many clergy with a reason to forsake any real attempt either to learn Irish or to use it in situations other than the strictly pastoral or catechetical. Thus they unwittingly assisted the creation of a situation by the end of the eighteenth century, when bilingualism was the norm throughout much of the country, and the foundations were in place for the rapid abandonment of the Irish language that occurred from the early decades of the nineteenth century onwards (164).

Bishops had considerable discretion in how they ran their dioceses. A minority – as well as numerous priests – were active in attending to the pastoral needs, notably in catechesis and preaching, of Irish-speaking Catholics, not least by providing texts suitable for pastoral use. For example, Bishop Michael O'Reilly (catechism, 1727), Bishop James Gallagher (sermons, 1736 – in strong demand throughout the country in the century after its publication), Bishop John O'Brien (dictionary, 1768), Dunleavy (catechism, 1742), and such priests as Tadhg Ó Conaill and John Heely (sermons) were notably active in the eighteenth century.

From the 1830s John McHale of Tuam became the leading member of the church hierarchy who publicly expressed, and practically demonstrated, support for the Irish language [Figures 5 and 6].[17] In the province of Connacht both Kirwin's catechism (1830) and McHale's catechism (1839) testified to the efforts of particular bishops to meet the practical pastoral needs of a largely Irish-speaking peasantry, and the evidence of the pre-Famine decades suggests that there was extensive catechetical instruction through Irish (with the assistance of lay instructors and using printed catechisms) (Mahon xxv-xxviii). These texts, and, in Cork, Muiris Paor's sermons and biblical commentary, are but the most significant examples of such clerical activity (Ní Mhurchú and Breathnach 141). Teachers in the "hedge" schools would sometimes teach catechism as well as the secular subjects (and sometimes both, in the chapel): indeed, some schoolmasters who worked for the Protestant Bible Societies were also to be found teaching their catechism to Catholics, their general linguistic usefulness allowing such "versatility."

For all that, it is difficult to argue with Brian Ó Cuív's summary of the general disposition of the Catholic Church of the era following the founding of the seminary at Maynooth:

there seems to be no evidence that the Irish hierarchy ever planned collectively to ensure that the clergy would be competent in both Irish and English. There were, of course, exceptions among the bishops, just as there were many priests who were fluent Irish speakers and used Irish in carrying out their religious duties, but the trend nationally and locally was to use English in church affairs – in public prayers, sermons, instructions, notices, inscriptions, church documents, and so on – except in circumstances where Latin would be the normal language ("Irish language and literature, 1845-1921" 392).

Yet it has been demonstrated that Maynooth's own clerical student body had a proportion of Irish speakers above the national average throughout the nineteenth century.[18] It wasn't competence, it seems, but attitude and habit that dictated their language use in their later parish work.

Furthermore, while some Catholic apologists in the early to mid-eighteenth century may have seen the Irish language as a bulwark of loyalty to Catholicism in its traditional, oral devotional culture among the peasantry, by the end of the century – and with the founding of Maynooth and other minor seminaries – such linguistic protectionist anxieties had largely vanished. They had been overtaken by the rising tide of Catholic self-confidence and of institutional expansion, especially among the Anglicized/Anglicizing Catholic urban middle class. Indeed, from the second quarter of the nineteenth century, as a strong revival of Protestant evangelical missions to the Irish poor focused some of its efforts (and resources) on the Irish-speaking poor of the western counties – and sought to evangelize these people in their own language – the aggressive response of the Catholic establishment seemed imbued with such a desire to keep their flock from straying that the Irish language itself might well be seen by some as something of a Trojan horse.[19] The fact that a number of local Irish scribes in different parts of the country found work as instructors in Irish for the bible societies further sharpened clerical anxieties.[20] Those respectable people (such as the scholar-antiquarian John O'Donovan) who evinced an interest in the spoken language and dressed in somber black clothing now risked becoming objects of suspicion, identified as potential proselytizers.[21]

Of course, the situation on the ground meant that many priests and some bishops continued to use Irish as a medium for direct contact with the poorer, Irish-speaking elements of their congregations, for common communication as well as for specifically pastoral purposes.[22] But among their own class (the Catholic bourgeoisie) or with the Protestant gentry, or in any dealings with an expanding "officialdom" (locally or, increasingly, centrally), English was their chosen medium. Indeed, their continuing use of Irish (for all that we find regular comments lamenting the decline of the ancient tongue and its rich store of experience and memory, including prayers and witness to God's presence in the everyday lives of the people) was generally seen as a temporary and transitional condition, pending the raising, through education, of the common people to civility, good order, and literacy in English. Indeed, as the idea gained credence that Ireland was destined to be the fountain for a Catholic spiritual empire across the English-speaking world (with the founding of All Hallows College in 1842), English became even more prized as the medium for this unique Irish Catholic missionary role.

Given these circumstances, it may be that MacMurchaidh's verdict: "Ultimately, as an institution, the Catholic Church's approach to Irish in the eighteenth century was at best neutral. Where it sought to address the language deficit, the attempt was frequently erratic and inconsistent" (187), may understate the active role that the Catholic Church played in the vernacular shift.

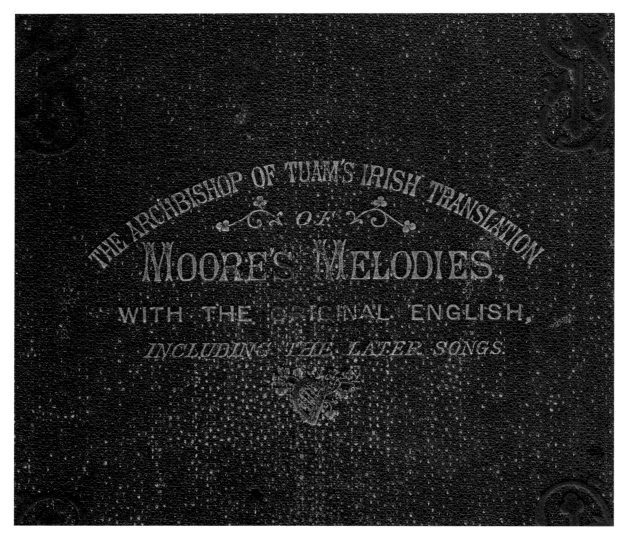

Figure 6 | John McHale, cover of *Moore's Melodies*

Among John McHale's published works was a translation into Irish of the popular *Moore's Melodies* by Thomas Moore.

PRAGMATISM & POWER

Recent scholarship has emphasized that the language shift in Ireland was, in a sense, a matter of pragmatism and choice, rather than being imposed coercively from the top. It is suggested that, in any consideration of the complexity of the language frontiers from the seventeenth to the early nineteenth century, it was a pragmatic choice for various strata of Irish society to adopt English, as opportunities presented themselves. In particular, it has been strongly argued that eighteenth-century Ireland was a bilingual society of considerable linguistic complexity. This proposition invites closer inspection. [23]

The limitations of Daniel Corkery's classic concept of a "Hidden Ireland" – in respect of his account of socio-economic conditions in eighteenth-century Munster – have been identified for some time. The notion – as it pertains to *mentalité* – of a sharply divided society, with its ruling classes functioning through English in all the key arteries of public life, and, as it were, an Irish-speaking underground or marginalized society, sustained and chronicled by poets for much of the period from the 1690s to the 1770s, has come under sustained attack again more recently. The immediate source of the renewed criticism of the idea of two language communities (and their literati), virtually hermetically sealed from each other, was an argument advanced by Joep Leerssen. Leerssen applied a version of Habermas's concept of the "public sphere" to the domains of Irish- and English-speaking Ireland in the eighteenth and early nineteenth centuries, and concluded that Irish lacked a public sphere: "Gaelic Ireland was atomized into many separate small-scale communities without the wherewithal to form a society, without the joint continuum of a public sphere" (*Hidden Ireland* 36-37). [24]

The response of Irish scholars to Leerssen has generally been critical. This has been partly on the grounds that Habermas's original model is inadequate or inappropriate and that multiple and overlapping social spheres would more accurately describe the language "market" in eighteenth-century Ireland. In particular, a number of scholars have demonstrated that there was considerable interchange across the two vernaculars between the print and manuscript sectors of Irish literary production;

that interest in manuscripts was significant among many educated consumers of English-language printed material; that Irish-language scribes were familiar with English-language reading material (books and newspapers); that some actually wrote in both languages; and that there was regular interpenetration of the two vernaculars (vocabulary, literary forms, etc.)[25] In short, it is suggested that throughout the eighteenth century Ireland was a more fluidly bilingual and richly diglossic society than the "Hidden Ireland/Irish" versus "public sphere/English" dichotomy allows for. The consensus endorses Niall Ó Ciosáin's earlier conclusion that "between 1750 and 1850 Ireland was at all points [...] an intensely bilingual and diglossic society" (*Print and Popular Culture* 6).

Certainly, the rich mosaic of linguistic and literary exchange between literati and scholars in both languages, which has emerged in recent scholarship, leaves little room for mutually exclusive language domains: and if we add the world of the commercial and social intercourse of the countryside, and the world of religious worship and popular devotion, clearly the story is one of considerable complexity. Yet, we may reasonably caution against a Whiggish interpretation of the underlying trajectory of language change as being a gradual, inexorable and, in a sense, voluntary and pragmatic choice in the interest of progress. The cultural exchange or intercourse between the two vernaculars – given the realities of power – cannot be judged as anything other than unequal and grossly asymmetrical. From the time of the Conquest, the law, politics and administration, indeed the entire state apparatus was conducted through English: legal documents, public announcements, proclamations, and the administration of justice were all in English. The immediate pre-Famine decades saw a huge expansion in the centralizing British state's direct dealings with the population at large.[26]

But the vernacular language shift had been in one direction only from as early as the seventeenth century. By the later eighteenth century Irish manuscripts may have been of interest to certain groups of educated English speakers, and in many areas of the country competence in Irish would probably have been a distinct advantage for landlords or their agents (or for peddlers, shopkeepers, customs officials, constabulary, or magistrates) in dealing with the lower peasantry. But English was the vernacular of the bourgeoisie (in town, and increasingly in country) of all denominations, in their public dealings and in their domestic lives. The monoglot Irish speaker was at a major disadvantage in his direct dealings with the state apparatus, for example in dealing with leases or summonses or other notices. The acquisition of English became an urgent need with the expanding net of communication (state, commercial, labor mobility), and the desire that the children would be proficient in English led to strong parental collusion with the private schools that worked to ensure that children be firmly discouraged from using Irish.[27]

Accordingly, the kind of bilingual society that operated in eighteenth- and early nineteenth-century Ireland was one in which the advance of English was taken for granted by all the elites and leaders (in state, civil society, commerce, and the "church of the people"), and in which the need for Irish – for commercial dealings with the lower peasantry, or for effective pastoral care – was seen as a temporary and diminishing need that would disappear over time, as educational opportunity improved and regular contact with the progressive society increased.

If, therefore, the notion of "pragmatic" or "realistic" choice is employed to emphasize that, in these later, decisive centuries of vernacular language shift, there was no explicit state policy to suppress Irish, to prohibit its use (in print or in spoken communication) or its transmission, then one could hardly quibble with the choice of adjectives. But in describing such a complex issue as language shift as starkly as "pragmatic," without reference to the structures of power and influence within which the shift took place, one runs the risk of seeing it as responding to an almost impersonal force of nature. The cultural "climate change" in modern Ireland, to which the adaptive response was a change in vernacular, was ideological and political, and had identifiable human agency.

On the evidence of linguistic and literary interchange and the ordinary needs of trade and commerce in rural society, we may see the point of Liam MacMathúna's conclusion: "The linguistic history of the eighteenth century also confirms Bhahba'a judgment that 'the borderline engagements of cultural difference may as often be consensual as conflictual' " ("Verisimilitude or subversion?" 138).[28] But language frontiers are never stable. And what needs emphasis in the Irish case is that the vernacular shift since the sixteenth century was entirely one-way: from Irish to English, with a bilingual state merely a staging post in the journey (and a relatively short one within "progressive" families) from one monolingual regime to another.[29]

What exactly, then, did a pragmatic choice mean in the historical context under consideration? A choice where Irish signified the past, stagnation, backwardness, an incapacity to advance, an incapacity to negotiate the law, authority, the state and its apparatuses, the expanding civic space (and, increasingly, the formal, institutional world of religious worship, duty, observance); and English signified competence, access to the future, opportunity, advancement, progress, the possibility of participation, and mobility – social as well as geographical. The terms of "choice" in these circumstances need careful consideration. Whether pragmatism altogether meets the predicament and its resolution must remain open to question. We may ponder Liam de Paor's observation that "cultures die no more easily than persons" (67).

Thus, for scribes and scholars copying or compiling manuscripts (and in many instances including new material, their own work or that of their contemporaries) and mixing with patrons, whether ascendancy collectors, learned institutions, Protestant divines, or Catholic patrons of the "middling sort," the world they inhabited was a bilingual one.[30] They were literate in both Irish and English; had

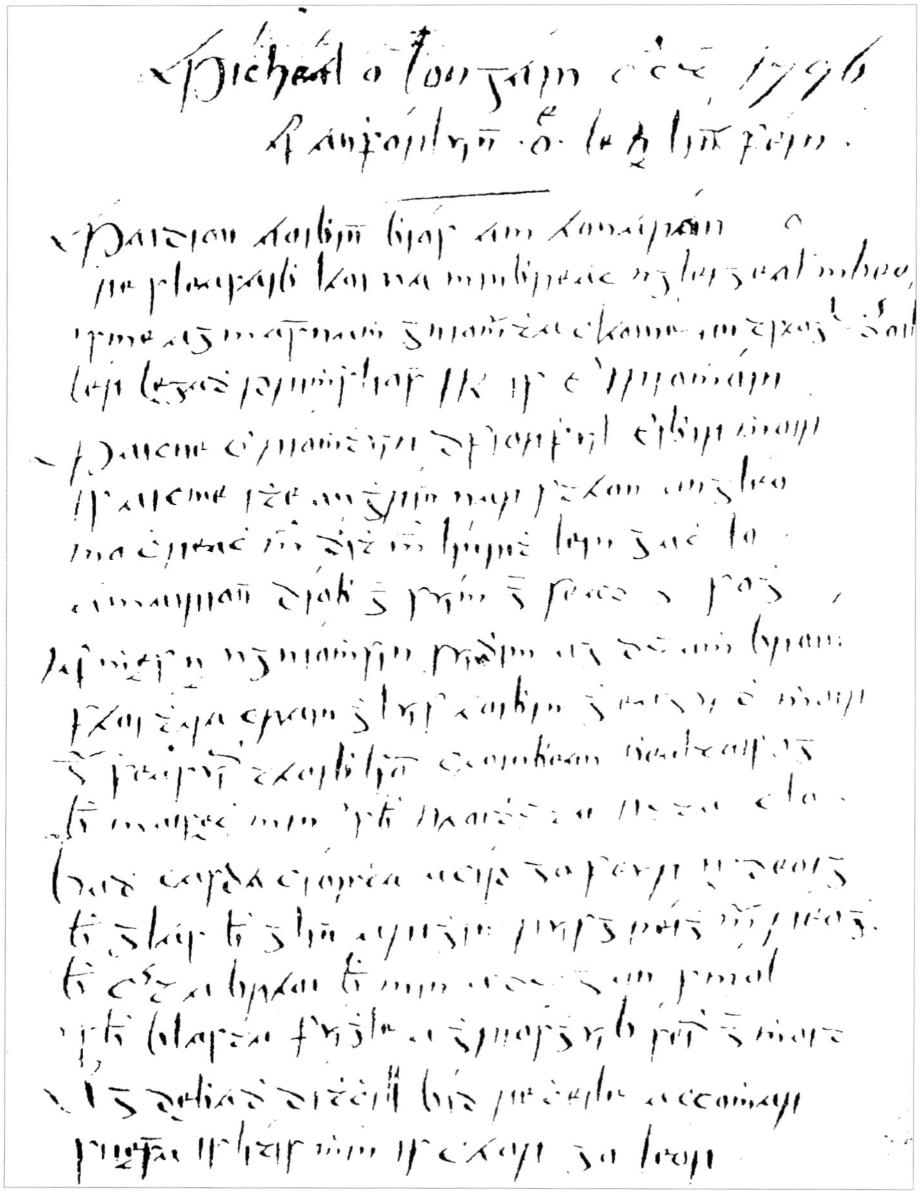

Figure 7 | Example of Gaelic script by Micheál Óg Ó Longáin (1796).

The compilation and circulation of manuscripts in Irish (copies of established work and original matter) by scribes remained vigorous right up to the eve of the Famine.

access to books and, as the eighteenth century advanced, newspapers in English; were *au fait* with political and other news in the public sphere; and were vital elements in the network of manuscript collection and production, which by the later eighteenth century was increasingly becoming a corpus of valued records of Irish history and antiquities in national institutions of the learned and enlightened scholars and patriots – the Royal Irish Academy and Trinity College Dublin being the main repositories in Ireland.

But for many of the agents of this literary activity in the production of Irish manuscripts, the language was seen as the vessel of an ancient and glorious literature and civilization. Certainly, it was worthy of being recorded and, if possible, worthy of steps being taken to ensure continued access to its inspiring riches (through translation or through the provision of dictionaries, grammars, and other aids to ensuring literacy in Irish). But, towards the actual contemporary speech community of Irish – for whom it was their principal and, for some, their only language – many scholars had a more ambiguous attitude. One might say that the more elevated their sense of their learned calling and scholarly competence (in reading and transcribing manuscripts, ancient history, and genealogy), the more likely were they to view the largely illiterate lower peasantry – who constituted the majority of the actual living speech community of Irish – with a certain condescension.

Thus, for all that he himself was an Irish speaker from childhood, and for all the outstanding corpus of scholarly work that he accomplished, there is no disguising the fact that John O'Donovan – the leading scholar-antiquarian of the Ordnance Survey and arguably of the entire nineteenth century – frequently displayed a dismissive attitude towards the generality of the Irish-speaking community from whom he sought to obtain topographical information. They were mainly illiterate, and he trusted manuscript sources over local informants on any obscure or contested topographical issue; above all, he held a skeptical opinion of the world-view and traditional beliefs and customs of these people (Ó Cadhla 33-169).[31] Stiofán Ó Cadhla's perceptive portrait of O'Donovan's general disposition is worth quoting: "His gaze is not always entirely innocent. At times it seems to be the same commanding and condescending eye of the colonizer. Occasionally he trains his vision on the vernacular culture of his own country within the parameters of colonialist discourse" (155).

Such attitudes mattered. Apart altogether from the pragmatic calculation of advantage in the language shift, in the social-psychological climate that had developed since the defeat of the Gaelic order and the establishment of the dominant English polity from the sixteenth century, the association of Irish with defeat, dispossession and – increasingly as population increased from the 1770s – poverty, further operated to make the social world of the actual Irish-speaking community one to escape from rather than join. Furthermore, while it is clear from contemporary reports that Irish was to be heard on the streets of the cities and towns well into the nineteenth century, yet there was no significant urban settlement (in pre-Famine decades) in which Irish was the dominant medium of social intercourse for all classes of the population, nor was it the ordinary medium for the developing culture of clubs, societies, and civic institutions of urban Ireland from the second quarter of the eighteenth century.[32]

The weak presence of Irish in the burgeoning print culture in Ireland (from the later seventeenth century) has been emphasized in recent scholarship. It has been established that "no Irish-language titles were published in Ireland between 1650 and 1700, and that between 1700 and 1750 only four Irish-language titles were published, compared to c. 9,000 titles in English" (Kelly and MacMurchaidh 29). Further, "a modest 19 Irish-language titles were published in Ireland between 1751 and 1800, and only 150 between 1801 and 1850." By contrast, some 16,000 English-language titles were published in Ireland during 1751–1800 (Kelly and MacMurchaidh 39, note 91). In fact, "printing in Irish peaked between 1800 and 1845, and collapsed thereafter" (Ó Ciosáin, "Pious miscellanies" 278). [33] Furthermore, printed books in Irish seem to have assumed a readership with prior literacy in English. [34]

Literacy, as reported officially in census returns, meant of course literacy in English. Self-reporting of competence carries inevitable risks. But the data suggest that in 1841 some forty-seven percent of those over five years old claimed to be able to read; by 1851 this had increased to fifty-three percent, and by 1911 it was close to ninety percent (Ó Gráda 240).

It has been suggested that "the weakness of print culture in Irish was partly counterbalanced by continuing manuscript activity" (Ó Ciosáin, "Pious miscellanies" 281). Certainly, Ó Cuív's figure of over 4,000 manuscripts in Irish dating from the eighteenth and nineteenth centuries (compared to 250 from the seventeenth) supports this view ("Irish Language and Literature, 1691–1845" 391). [35] But the fact that the production and distribution of manuscripts was vigorous during that period, and that courts of poetry met from time to time in different areas where manuscript compilation and composition in Irish remained vigorous, can hardly be considered as constituting that critical mass, density, and "continuous sphere of communication" that might merit classification as an alternative public sphere to that occupied by English.

That the public sphere might be re-occupied by the Catholic "nation," but in no significant degree by the Irish language, is evident in the political mass-mobilization movements of Daniel O'Connell. Indeed, for many, O'Connell's mass politics in the second quarter of the century was a decisive episode in the language shift (and O'Connell's own indifference, on utilitarian grounds – to put it no more strongly – to the survival of Irish is well known) (MacDonagh 8–14). [36] Later popular movements – such as the Fenians (largely town-centered), the Land War, the Parnellite movement for Home Rule, and in sport (the GAA) – all reflected and further consolidated the dominance of English, though individual leaders in all such movements can be identified who gave some obeisance to the importance of the Irish language in affirming Irish nationality.

Geographically, the language shift was largely determined by the rate (and timing) of the absorption of the more inaccessible western districts into "national" politics and regulated religious devotion, as well as the retail network, the world of the "shop" and the commercial traveler, the barracks, the revenue, the coast guard, and

Figure 8 | Frederic William Burton, *Thomas Osborne Davis (1814-1845), Poet and Politician*

Thomas Davis, writer and cultural nationalist, advocated preservation and use of the Irish language as an essential mark of Irish nationality.

the national school. While these domestic drivers of the vernacular language shift were operating in most of the arteries of Irish life, emigration, both seasonal and permanent, was a further potent source of changing aspirations and attitudes. In the post-Famine decades, the still strongly Irish-speaking areas of the west became inexorably absorbed into the grid of communications and mobility for which English was desirable or necessary, and within which Irish was increasingly perceived as obsolete and without transactional value.

In sum, taking the total social context into account, and leaving aside Leerssen's overly schematic binary terms of "Hidden Ireland, Public Sphere," his contention that by the eighteenth and early nineteenth centuries the Irish language lacked a public sphere raises complex questions regarding the absence or exclusion of Irish from the vital structures and domains of civil society in pre-Famine Ireland.

AGAINST THE TIDE

The seemingly relentless march of English through the countryside is not, however, the whole story of the pre-Famine decades. In several areas there were active networks of scribes and scholars – copying, compiling, and composing new material in Irish. In Belfast a circle centered on the businessman William McAdam and Dr. James McDonnell constituted itself as Cuideacht Gaedhilge Uladh (founded in 1830), whose projects included manuscript commissioning and collection, and practical schemes for acquiring Irish formally through primers and Irish classes. [37] These activities may be traced to the current of intellectual interest in acquiring knowledge of the native culture that was an aspect of Belfast civic enlightenment of the late eighteenth century. The Cuideacht also planned to start non-denominational schools in which Irish would be taught, in Tyrone, Derry, and Donegal **[Figure 9]**. [38]

McAdam's suppliers of manuscripts included a number of scribes active in a wedge (still with a significant number of Irish speakers) running from County Louth across to north Meath and pockets of Monaghan, who combined scribal work with teaching and whose own compositions were frequently socially engaged and of genuine literary merit. [39] In County Cork, a lively cohort of scribes, including the Ó Longáins and Donncha Ó Floinn, patronized by clergy and by comfortable Catholics, also had contact with men like Cork antiquarian John Windele and Thomas Swanton in West Cork, a Protestant with a lively interest in the cultivation and transmission of the living language by practical schemes. [40] In Waterford, Philip Barron established a short-lived, Irish-medium school, and launched a clutch of Irish publications (Breathnach and Ní Mhurchú 17–18). These were the kind of people who would later be described as "language activists."

In south Tipperary, south Kilkenny, and parts of Waterford, an active network of scribes and scholars of Irish not only produced an impressive volume of manuscript material but were also active in a number of printing projects, only some of which came to fruition. [41] The more scholarly of these were in communication with metropolitan institutions such as the Royal Irish Academy, while a wide circle of these scribes had contact with the antiquarian scholar James Hardiman, in his

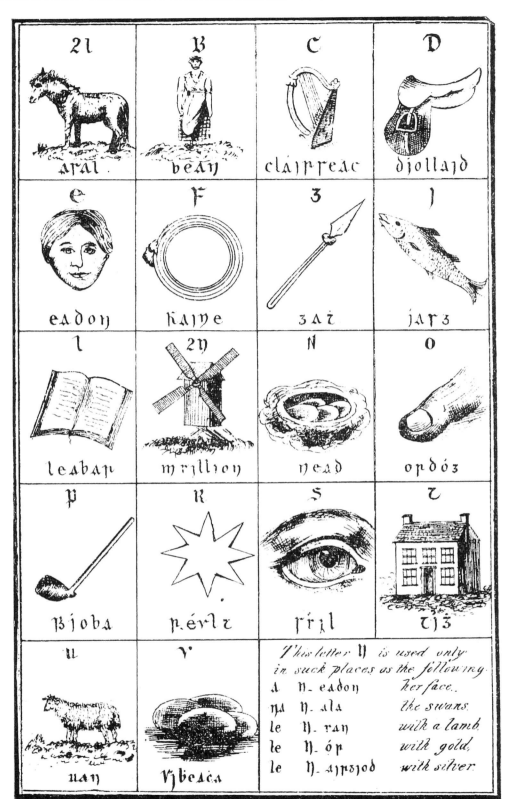

Figure 9 | Page from an Irish primer.

One of the publications of the pre-Famine Belfast-based society Cuideacht Gaedhilge Uladh, dedicated to promoting the cultivation and use of the Irish language.

compiling of the influential *Irish Minstrelsy* (two volumes published in 1831). Indeed, even in Connacht (the least active province in respect of the later manuscript tradition), Hardiman was familiar with the contemporary blind popular poet Antoine Raiftearaí, some of whose compositions would survive both in manuscript and through oral transmission. [42] And these are only the most notable examples. [43]

Furthermore, and vitally, the language itself (as the surviving corpus of literature composed in it clearly testifies) remained vigorous, innovative, and "engaged" with contemporary society, even as the social condition of its speakers declined. [44] Additionally, it encoded and transmitted an historical consciousness based on such key canonical texts as Keating's *Foras Feasa ar Éirinn* and the long historical poem *Tuireamh na hÉireann*, as well as a strong vein of composition in manuscript form, some of which would also be transmitted orally to later generations. [45]

Nevertheless, this lively scribal activity of the immediate pre-Famine decades did not indicate any kind of reversal of the underlying shift to English among the ambitious young and those availing of any kind of elementary education or better. Indeed, the fatalism that marked the attitudes of even the most accomplished scribes is captured by Micheál Ó Raghallaigh of Ennistymon, County Clare, who continued compiling manuscripts right up to the Famine:

A léitheoir ionúin, ná tabhair aithis ná milleán orm trí olcas an scríbhinn atá sa leabhar seo. Óir is fear ceirde mé, agus is in aimsir dhíomhaoin a rinné mé an cnuasach seo. Dá bhrí sin, an tan a chonacthas dom nach raibh aon duine de lucht mo chomhaimsire ag cnuasach a bheag de shaothar ár bhfilí, mheas mé gan iad uile a ligean ar fán. Ach is beag an tairbhe iad a chosaint, óir is náireach lenár n-aos óg teanga a sinsear a fhoghluim. Dá bhrí sin ní bhia focal Gaeilge sa ríocht i gceann céad bliain eile má leanaid an nós atá acu lem'chuimhne féin (Ó Fiannachta 98). [46]

The dominant note here – as frequently with scribes and scholars – is one of anxiety and largely one of resignation: that the task upon which they were embarked was an important and (in terms of Ireland's past) a culturally worthy task; but that unless a major reversal took place in public attitudes, especially among the rising generation, the language was doomed – a great shame and a form of historical apostasy, but inevitable. Even writers who, exceptionally, confided their intimate thoughts and feelings to paper in Irish – like the Callan shopkeeper and schoolmaster diarist Amhlaoibh Ó Súilleabháin – did so while accepting the desirability of the advance of the Victorian respectable virtues and deportment for which English was the appropriate and the triumphant medium. [47] Maureen Wall's memorable verdict on the note of linguistic fatalism that underpins the Catholic leadership in general as it presided over the vernacular language shift at an accelerating rate from the early nineteenth century, even as its own all-encompassing infrastructure of socialization fortified communal identity based on religious loyalty, is worth quoting: "This note of *auld lang syne* so commonly heard during the eighteenth and nineteenth centuries, when Irish was still spoken by a large part of the population, was one factor in hastening the decay of the language" (Wall 84). To what extent such fatalism affected language use among Irish speakers busy with their daily lives it is impossible to say, but it clearly influenced the language that they wished their children to speak. [48]

Whether we situate the language shift from the outset within the discourse of colonialism, or, following the assimilation of an indigenous (Catholic) bourgeoisie into the Anglophone polity and culture, in broadly Gramscian terms of hegemony, the brute fact was that by the eve of the Famine the cultural/linguistic logic of conquest (and of assimilation into an "open" economy, a centralized state with virtually ubiquitous outreach, and an Anglophone world for which mass Irish emigration was increasingly destined) was fully grasped by all classes of Irish society. Moreover, as communications, trade, and literacy all contributed to increased mobility, the opportunities for acting on that logic had begun to penetrate into the remoter regions and the most depressed social groups in society. It would be later in the century before the emigration rates from Connacht outran the national average and the state's targeted initiatives (through the Congested Districts Board) made sustained impact on life in the contracting western Irish-speaking areas or *Gaeltachtaí*; but whatever protection geographical remoteness or poverty may have provided for Irish was already well on the way to being undermined by the eve of the Famine. [49]

POST-FAMINE PERSPECTIVES

The Famine decimated the rural underclass which was the mainstay of Irish-speaking Ireland. In the decades that followed, the abandonment of Irish and the adoption of English proceeded apace. The figures (see Table A) indicate the pattern. There were new factors that further accelerated the shift that was already well under way by 1841. The coming of the railways from the 1850s further integrated the rural economy and society into the retail network, and further increased mobility, both internally and for emigration. The expansion in the infrastructure of the Catholic Church – with increased personnel and new schools and convents – furthered the spread of English. Emigration – the single most vital fact of Irish social history in recent centuries – was predominantly to the Anglophone world, and from the final quarter of the nineteenth century the rate of emigration from the western counties of Ireland (to which the Irish language was increasingly retreating) overtook the national average rate, thus providing a further incentive, if one were needed, to acquire English (Fitzpatrick 9–13) **[Figure 10]**. The shame of the rising generation (voiced by Ó Raghallaigh) may have been exacerbated by the horror of the Famine experience, where Irish was on the lips of the underclass dying in ditches or heading to the poorhouse. Indeed, the death of the Meath-born Irish writer and scribe Aodh Mac Domhnaill, in Cootehill workhouse in 1867, is invoked by Máirtín Ó Cadhain as the shameful defining image of language loss in the nineteenth century (52).

The precise role of the Famine in the process of language shift, and in deeper patterns of cultural change in modern Ireland, has elicited challenging responses from a number of historians and critics. In 1965 Seán de Fréine proposed that the rupture of the continuity of a national community (bonded by a shared language and sense of shared peoplehood) produced disorientation and forms of individual and social anomie that had a profound and disabling effect on all later efforts at national endeavor and collective purpose. For de Fréine, this disorientation caused by language loss preceded the Famine and, to some degree, rendered Irish society incapable of dealing effectively with that calamity (5–32). More recently, both Tony Crowley and Angela Bourke, in assessing the more long-term consequences of the language shift, attributed particular significance to the Famine. Thus, for Crowley:

migration and emigration to English-speaking places do not explain fully the effect of the Famine on the use of Irish. The sheer psychological and cultural impact of the experience of mass starvation is one factor which must be counted as part of any explanation. The sense of helplessness, loss, panic, and uncertainty, perhaps combined with a determination to avoid such a disaster at all costs in the future, no doubt helped to undermine even the most traditional communities (War of Words 121).

There is an echo here of Sir William Wilde's claim in 1852 that "the festivals are unobserved, the rustic festivities neglected or forgotten." Traditional beliefs, superstitions, cures, customs, and remedies, their protective magic having failed cruelly during the Famine, were being abandoned. The fairies were giving way to "the schoolmaster and the railroad engineer" (qtd. in Malcolm 40).

Bourke, in counting the cost of the loss of Irish, claims that "the nineteenth-century ideology of rationality, with its linear and colonial thought-patterns, gained ascendancy over a vernacular cognitive system in Ireland, especially after the Famine." Referring to "the great cultural shifts which followed the Famine in Ireland," she draws attention to "the rich resources of imagination, memory, creativity and communication that were jettisoned when the Irish language and its oral traditions were denigrated and discarded throughout much of the country" (79). Seán Connolly traces the "beginnings of a revolution in mentalities" to the 1820s and 1830s, a process "massively accelerated by the particular havoc which the Famine of 1845-50 wreaked on those sections of the population among whom traditional practices and beliefs, as well as Irish language speaking, had remained strongest" (109-110). This view is consistent with accounts of the widespread abandonment of traditional practices recorded by contemporaries (including the letters of the Ordnance Survey officers) in the generation before the Famine (Ó Cadhla 133-169).

Whatever view we take of such deeper cultural mutations, what is incontrovertible is that the post-Famine decades would see an acceleration in the abandonment of Irish for English among the population at large. There were isolated acts of resistance, including some undertaken by emigrants. Phrases in Irish appeared in nationalist newspapers in Ireland and among exiles in the post-Famine decades: the *Nation* (from 1859), the *Irish-American* in New York (from 1869 – in which Uilleog de Búrca's *Easy Lessons in Irish* were reprinted); the *Tuam News* and the *Tuam Herald*; the *Shamrock* (1872 to 1875); and in letters to the *Irish World* in the early 1870s recommending revival (Ó Cadhain 52). Then in 1874 Mícheál Ó Lócháin, a Galway exile, started in Brooklyn the Philo-Celtic societies that would spread throughout the USA, and in 1881 established *An Gaodhal*, a monthly bilingual magazine **[Figure 11]**. [50]

In 1862 Richard D'Alton (1814-75) of Tipperary town, a Young Irelander, baker, and republican, founded a short-lived (seven issues) journal, entitled, as its first edition on March 17, 1862 announced: "*An Fíor Éirionach: The First Move to the Restoration of the Irish Language*. To be printed in weekly numbers, containing Catholic prayers and selections from the poetry and history of our country" (qtd. in Ní Mhurchú and Breathnach 37-8). A vital transitional figure across the Famine divide is John O'Daly (1800-78). Born in Waterford, his early involvement (in Kilkenny) with the Irish (Bible) Society's activity, and later through his bookshop, was accompanied by antiquarian and language activism, culminating in his 1844 publication, *Reliques of Irish Jacobite Poetry*. Moving to Dublin in 1845, he busied himself as Secretary to the Celtic Society (1845) and the later Ossianic Society (1855), and published numerous Irish texts, not only through devotion to literary "reliques" but also Uilleog de Búrca's *The College Irish Grammar* in 1856 and Tadhg Gaelach Ó Súilleabháin's *Pious Miscellany* in 1868 (Ní Mhurchú and Breathnach 98-100) **[Figure 12]**.[51] In the west, Archbishop McHale and his kinsman Fr. Uilleog de Búrca had significant influence, radiating from Tuam across the Famine divide and providing a vital bridge to the revival impulse of the final quarter of the century. Moreover, these Tuam activists were operating in an area where the Irish language was still strong among the common people of the countryside.[52]

The Famine's impact was felt throughout all corners of the traumatized and demoralized world of Irish – its scholars, scribes, schoolmasters and speakers. In Belfast – as McAdam's business began to fail and the Protestant commitment to civic culture started to flow into new channels – the interest in cultivating the native language and culture, which had been evident from the later eighteenth century, began to weaken. The outer reaches of McAdam's patronage – not least in north Leinster and south-east Ulster – registered the contraction, as we may trace in the career of Peadar Ó Gealacáin (1792-1860). Born in Moynalty, County Meath, well-educated – evidently in a good hedge school – Ó Gealacáin was a traveling schoolmaster and scribe. Teaching for a time with the Irish (Protestant) Bible Society, while copying and compiling a large corpus and wide variety of manuscripts and notes in a good hand, Ó Gealacáin's manuscript production was mainly in the years 1822-54, until McAdam's business declined and his patronage dropped off.[53] He found a few patrons among the Gaelic Society in Drogheda until his death in 1860.

Manuscript copying did not cease altogether with the Famine, but it tapered off sharply thereafter. We can only guess at the number of manuscripts lost in the chaos of death and dispersal that attended the great calamity, or indeed the number that crossed the seas with emigrants in these and later years. The more humble of the scribes felt the fatal pull of the ebbing tide, though several (e.g. the Ó Longáins of Cork) would find part-time work in various editorial tasks for the Royal Irish Academy.[54] The senior scholars and antiquarians ensured that the scholarly editing, translation, and publishing of the important manuscripts from an earlier era would continue, mainly under the auspices of learned societies. The very years that would see tens of thousands of Irish speakers die of hunger and disease would also see the publication (six volumes, 1848-51) of John O'Donovan's magnificent edition of the *Annals of the Four Masters*.

Figure 11 | *Cover of An Gaodhal* (April, 1884)

The bilingual monthly journal *An Gaodhal* was launched in New York in 1881 by the Galway-born emigrant, Micheál Ó Lócháin.

O'Donovan would continue to publish scholarly editions of important Irish manuscript material and would receive acknowledgment (though neither students nor income) by appointment to the Chair of Celtic at Queen's University Belfast. Eoghan O'Curry, likewise, would pursue his antiquarian and historical researches, as paid professor at Cardinal Newman's new Catholic university in Dublin, until his death in 1862. [55] The antiquarian societies active from the 1840s mainly involved the metropolitan-based intelligentsia, though the membership of the Ossianic Society (founded 1853) came from a wider geographical area, notably the Munster towns, and seems to have attracted support from lower-middle and artisan classes. It also seems to have seen its activities as contributing, *inter alia*, to the preservation of Irish as a living language (Murray 86-95). But a concerted effort at revival would not come until later in the century.

What remains a puzzling question, of course, is why the acquisition of English led – within a few generations – to the abandonment of Irish: why more sustained, fluid forms of bilingualism did not take hold. Here the die was probably cast at a

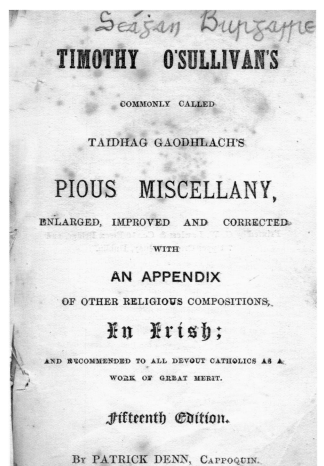

Figure 12 | Cover of *Pious Miscellany* by Timothy O'Sullivan (Tadhg Gaelach Ó Súilleabháin)

The most popular and frequently-printed devotional work in Irish was Timothy O'Sullivan's (Tadhg Gaelach Ó Súilleabháin) *Pious Miscellany*, first published in 1802.

relatively early stage, so far as attitudes were concerned. When the leaders of the Irish-speaking majority were eclipsed or forced into exile, or when they elected to culturally (if not necessarily religiously) conform to the new order, the close association of Irish with defeat, demoralization, and, in time, poverty and shame became deeply embedded. Thereafter, the common people would have needed alternative leadership or formidable insulation from the institutions of the new order if they were not to imbibe the same attitudes towards the two vernaculars as the advancing Catholic bourgeoisie had clearly adopted. In this context, the role of the Catholic Church in the language shift assumes particular importance. It was the only institution across the island in which the old leadership (whether of Gaelic or old English stock) retained control and which held the people's loyalty and provided a vital site of communal solidarity, socialization, and affirmation of identity for the majority population.

But to the wider question of why the acquisition of English meant, overwhelmingly, the abandonment of Irish, answers may be better sought in the study of collective behavior rather than simply in a multitude of "rational" individual choices. The emotional impact on a family or household of suppressing or expelling a language and replacing it with another – the inter-generational ruptures involved – must have been sharply disruptive, however rational the motivation for the change. Again, we can only imagine (or trust the dramatist or the novelist to realize for us) what the acoustic reality and social-psychological drama of these individual and collective attitudes may have produced in an individual dwelling, or in the chapel, shop, school, or square of a market town on a fair day in, say, the second quarter of the nineteenth century. [56]

SURVIVAL/REVIVAL?

But, for all that, as the population of Irish speakers continued to fall in the decades after 1851, the geographical retreat of Irish to the Atlantic seaboard continued, with a cluster of enclaves holding out against all the odds. And, as the wedges of monoglot English-speaking areas widened, so too did the dialect differences between the now-divided Irish-speaking areas become ever more pronounced.

Within a generation of the Great Famine the imminent death of Irish as a living language was being forecast, not (as in the aftermath of the conquest and colonization of earlier centuries) by fallen mandarins of a defeated and exiled elite, nor indeed by the anxious poets, patriotic antiquarians or evangelizing cultural nationalists of the late eighteenth and early nineteenth centuries, but in the commentaries of schools inspectors and in the dry language of the numerate bureaucrat. In 1856 the humane educationalist, P. J. Keenan, explained the passion for education of the (overwhelmingly Irish-speaking) people on the islands off the Donegal coast in unambiguous terms:

this strong passion for education [...] may be traced to one predominant desire – the desire to speak English. They see, whenever a stranger visits their islands, that prosperity has its peculiar tongue as well as its fine coat; they see that while the traffickers who occasionally approach them to deal in fish, or in kelp, or in food, display the yellow gold, they count it out in English; and if they ever cross over to the mainland for the 'law', as they call any legal process, they see that the solemn words of judgment have to come second to them, through the offices of an interpreter. [...] and whilst they may love the cadences, and mellowness, and homeliness of the language which their fathers gave them, they yet see that obscurity and poverty distinguish their lot from the English-speaking people; and, accordingly, no matter what the sacrifice to their feelings, they long for the acquisition of the 'new tongue', with all its prizes and social privileges. The keystone of fortune is the power of speaking English (qtd. in Crowley, *The Politics of Language in Ireland: 1366-1922* 165).

The writer of the Preface to the 1871 census report was clear on the inevitable outcome of the story: "The disappearance of this ancient member of the Celtic family of tongues from living speech may be somewhat delayed or somewhat accelerated by circumstances beyond calculation or conjecture, but there can be no error in the belief that within relatively a few years [sic] Irish will have taken its place among the languages that have ceased to exist" (qtd. in Hindley 20).

Yet, before that decade was out, there were calls to action to ensure the survival of Irish as a living language, culminating in the founding of the Society for the Preservation of the Irish Language (SPIL) in 1876. [57] Securing a footing for Irish within the education system was a priority for the new preservationists: the formal transmission of the language in the schools was a prerequisite for its survival, as it would combine enhanced status with basic literacy. There were educationalists who – on general pedagogic and learning-outcome grounds – had questioned the total exclusion of Irish (as a medium) from the education of children from Irish-speaking homes. Thus, Keenan informed the Commissioners of Education in 1879: "The real policy of the educationist would, in my opinion, be to teach Irish grammatically and soundly to the Irish-speaking people, and then to teach them English through the medium of their native language" (qtd. in Crowley, *The Politics of Language in Ireland:1366-1922* 181).

The lobbying of SPIL had modest success, and the further objective of publishing Irish literature and folklore of the living Irish-language community was advanced with the launch of *Irisleabhar na Gaeilge* in 1882. With the founding of the Gaelic League in 1893, survival had been joined by revival in the objectives regarding Irish as a living language. By the close of the century a new wave of cultural revival, encompassing folklore, literature, and the arts and crafts, together with an intense debate on Irish "national identity" – on which the political demand for an Irish national state was predicated – had seized the imagination of a younger generation. The demands for the Irish language's restoration to the public sphere became more ambitious, even as the actual community of native Irish speakers continued to decline, due to emigration and the continuing shift to English. By the early years of the twentieth century, the Irish language was becoming firmly embedded in the education system, and across a spectrum of political opinion expressions of support for its survival and for the extension of its use became commonplace. These sentiments were expressed with particular conviction by a minority of advanced nationalists. However, in the light of the centuries-long shift to English as the main vernacular of the country, and the global reach of English for what had become a diasporic people, by the time a cohort of advanced nationalists set out to restore Irish as the main vernacular of an Irish national state, it was very late in the day.

ENDNOTES

[1] See J. J. Lee, "On the accuracy of the pre-Famine Irish censuses," in J. M. Goldstrom and L. A. Clarkson (eds), *Irish Population, Economy and Society* (Oxford, 1981), pp 37-56

[2] See Crowley et al.

[3] In Crowley et al., Máiréad Nic Craith comments briefly on language loss (580-89); Neil Buttimer provides an original exploration of "The Great Famine in Gaelic Manuscripts" (460-472).

[4] See Ó Gliasáin 15 for adjusted 1851 estimate. It would be futile to seek to quantify distortions based on social-psychological factors.

[5] For earlier estimates see Ó Cuív, *Irish Dialects* 7-32.

[6] See de Paor 168 (a commentary on Fitgerald's figures).

[7] The most comprehensive historical surveys are found in Ó Cuív, "The Irish language in the early modern period," "Irish language and literature, 1691-1845," and "Irish language and literature, 1845-1921." For ideological analysis see, Morley; Palmer; Cunningham; and Canny.

[8] For a masterly exploration of the Gaelic Irish sentiment and aspirations for a Jacobite revival, see Ó Buachalla, *Aisling Ghéar*.

[9] See Ó Buachalla, *Aisling Ghéar*, and for further consideration, Ó Ciardha.

[10] For expanding state influence, Ó Tuathaigh 80-116; and Crossman.

[11] For discussion of the language dimension of popular literacy, see the ground-breaking Daly and Dickson; and the indispensable Ó Ciosáin, *Print and popular Culture*; also McManus.

[12] See Daly, "The Development of the National School System."

[13] See Akenson.

[14] On indifferent attendance rates and modest standards, see Mary E. Daly, *Social and Economic History* 111-118.

[15] The main "teaching" orders were the Presentation nuns (founded 1802 by Nano Nagle), the Mercy nuns (founded by Catherine McAuley and formally constituted 1820), and the Irish Christian Brothers (founded by Edmund Rice and formally constituted in 1820).

[16] See Cunningham; and Morley.

[17] A full-length scholarly biography of McHale is needed; but for valuable context, see Hoban; and Ó Muraíle, "Staid na Gaeilge."

[18] See Wolf, "The Irish-Speaking Clergy." It wasn't until after 1850 that Maynooth-educated clergy constituted a majority of Irish priests. A more expansive later treatment is Wolf, *An Irish-Speaking Ireland*.

[19] See Irene Whelan.

[20] See de Brún; also, for continuing tensions, Moffett.

[21] See O'Donovan's comments on the suspicion he aroused in Cavan in 1836, quoted in Ó Buachalla, *Cathal Buí* 31.

[22] The sacrament of Penance – Confession – was, understandably, especially sensitive in this context.

[23] This view permeates the Kelly and MacMurchaidh volume; for a review of which see Brian Ó Conchubhair, in *Irish Economic and Social History*, Vol. XXXX (2013): 156-160.

[24] See also the author's scintillating exploration of "the idea of Irish nationality" in *Mere Irish and Fíor-Ghael*.

[25] As the Introduction to the Kelly and MacMurchaidh volume concludes: "In sum, the relationship in which Irish and English were bound in the seventeenth, eighteenth and nineteenth centuries was more complex, more contingent and more intertwined than has been habitually portrayed prior to the recent surge in scholarship into language, print and culture" (41).

[26] A centralized system of policing and education, a new network of workhouses for Poor Relief, enhanced public works coordination, together with improved communications and travel conditions: all of these developments from the 1820s drew the population increasingly into direct contact with the state apparatus.

[27] For late survival of such collusion, see Máirtín 201-232.

[28] For an extended discussion of code-mixing, see the same author's *Béarla sa Ghaeilge*.

[29] The family of Daniel O'Connell in south-west Kerry provides a good example of the language shift: see MacDonagh 7-29.

[30] This Catholic "middling sort" of the eighteenth century is described by Morley as "a middle stratum of comfortable tenant farmers, craftsmen, schoolteachers, publicans, shopkeepers and priests, a stratum which was increasingly literate in English and which maintained a vigorous oral and manuscript-based literature in Irish" (qtd. in Kelly and MacMurchaidh 221).

[31] For an assured appraisal of O'Donovan the scholar, see Ó Muraíle, "Seán Ó Donnabháin."

[32] See Kelly Powell.

[33] The Irish figure is a small fraction of what was published in Welsh and only ten percent to fifteen percent of what was published in Scots Gaelic. No book in Irish was published in North America during the nineteenth century (Ó Ciosáin 277).

[34] See Cullen, "Patrons, teachers and literacy."

[35] Ó Cuív, "The Irish Language in the Early Modern Period" 391.

[36] For a sympathetic discussion of the Gaelic dimension of O'Connell, see Murphy.

[37] See Ó Buachalla, *I mBéal Feirste*.

[38] Maria Edgeworth gave the Cuideachta permission for two of her stories to be translated into Irish (Ó Buachalla, *I mBéal Feirste* 85-6).

[39] See, for example, Ó Fiaich and Ó Caithnia; Beckett; Ní Mhunghaile; and Smith.

[40] See Ó Chonchúr; Buttimer; Nic Craith.

[41] For the Tipperary-Kilkenny network, see Ó hÓgáin, *Duanaire Osraíoch* and *Duanaire Thiobraid Árann*; Ó Néill; and Ua Cearnaigh. The Irish book most in demand in the pre-Famine period, Tadhg Gaelach Ó Súilleabháin's *Pious Miscellany*, was first published in Clonmel in 1802, running to 18 editions by 1850 (Ó Ciosáin, "Pious miscellanies" 272).

[42] See Cullen, "Filíocht, Cultúr agus Polaitíocht"; and Ó Coigligh.

[43] See, for example, Madagáin; and essays on Clare and Connacht by, respectively, Eilís Ní Dheá and Nollaig Ó Muraíle, in Ó hUiginn. Indeed, virtually all the volumes in the county series *History and Society* contain valuable essays on the Irish language heritage in each county.

[44] See Ó Buachalla, "Canóin na Creille"; and Denvir.

[45] For the "cultural transfer" of this Gaelic historical consciousness to English-language nationalist rhetoric and historical narrative, see, from different perspectives, Leerssen, *Hidden Ireland* 13-27; and Morley 223-268.

[46] Translation: "Dear reader, Do not reproach or criticize me for the defects of the writing in this book. As I am a tradesman, it is in my spare time that I have made this collection. Accordingly, it could not be as accomplished as the work of a true scribe. But, for all that, when I saw that none of my contemporaries was collecting any of the work of our poets, I determined not to allow them to sink into oblivion. But it is a fruitless task trying to conserve them, as our young generation are ashamed to learn their ancestral language. Accordingly, if the practice that I have seen in my time continues, there will not be a word of Irish in this kingdom a hundred years from now."

[47] See Ó Drisceoil, *Ar Scaradh Gabhail*; and Liam P. Ó Murchú.

[48] The issue of gender in the language-shift – specifically, the influence of mothers on their children within the home – awaits close investigation.

[49] See Breathnach.

[50] See Ó Buachalla, "An Gaodhal' i Meiriceá"; and Uí Fhlannagáin. Ó Lóchain died in 1899 but the magazine survived until 1904.

[51] See also Ó Drisceoil, "Lámhscríbhinní agus an Léitheoir Coitianta."

[52] See note 17 above; also entry on "Seán Mac Fhlainn" (1843-1915), in Ní Mhurchú and Breathnach 53-54; and Ó Maolmhuaidh.

[53] See Dawson.

[54] See Ní Úrdail; and Ó Donnchadha.

[55] See Ó Fiannachta, *Ómós do Eoghan Ó Comhraí*.

[56] Case studies – closely observed – offer possibilities: see Ní Mhóráin. Ó Ciosáin's original approach – going beyond simple economic or ideological determinism – explores language-use as a cultural practice, with its own context-bound rules and conventions: see "Gaelic Culture and Language Shift."

[57] See Máirtín Ó Murchú.

WORKS CITED

Akenson, Donald H. *The Irish Education Experiment*. London: Routledge and Kegan Paul, 1970.

Beckett, Colm, ed. *Aodh Mac Domhnaill: Dánta*. Dublin: Clóchomhar, 1987.

Bourke, Angela. "The Baby and the Bathwater." *Ideology and Ireland in the Nineteenth Century*. Ed. Tadhg Foley and Seán Ryder. Dublin: Four Courts, 1998. 79-92.

Breathnach, Ciara. *The Congested Districts Board 1891-1923*. Dublin: Four Courts, 2005.

Breathnach, Diarmuid and Máire Ní Mhurchú, eds. *Beathaisnéis*. 9 vols. Dublin: Clóchomhar, 1986-2007.

Buttimer, Neil. "Gaelic literature and contemporary life in Cork, 1700-1840." *Cork: History & Society*. Ed. Neil Buttimer and Patrick O'Flanagan. Dublin: Geography Publications, 1993. 585-653.

Canny, Nicholas. "The Formation of the Irish Mind: Religion, Politics and Gaelic Irish Literature, 1580-1750." *Past and Present* 95 (May 1982): 91-116.

Connolly, Seán. "Popular Culture." *Conflict, Identity and Economic Development: Ireland and Scotland, 1600-1939*. Ed. S. J. Connolly, R. A. Houston, and R. J. Morris. Preston: Carnegie, 1995. 103-113.

Crossman, Virginia. *Politics, Law and Order in Nineteenth-Century Ireland*. Dublin: Gill & Macmillan, 1996.

Crowley, John, William J. Smyth, and Mike Murphy, eds. *Atlas of the Great Irish Famine*. Cork: Cork UP, 2012.

Crowley, Tony. *The Politics of Language in Ireland: 1366-1922*. London: Routledge, 2000.

---. *War of Words: The Politics of Language in Ireland: 1537-2004*. Oxford: OUP, 2005.

Cullen, Louis M. "Filíocht, Cultúr agus Polaitíocht." *Nua-Léamha: Gnéithe de Chultúr, Stair agus Polaitíocht na hÉireann, c.1600-c.1900*. Ed. Máirín Ní Dhonnchadha. Dublin: Clóchomhar, 1996. 170-199.

---."Patrons, teachers and literacy in Irish, 1700-1850." Daly and Dickson 15-44.

Cunningham, Bernadette. *The World of Geoffrey Keating: History, Myth and Religion in Seventeenth-Century Ireland*. Dublin: Four Courts, 2000.

Daly, Mary E. *Social and Economic History of Ireland Since 1800*. Dublin: The Educational Company, 1981.

---. "The Development of the National School System, 1831-40." Ed. Art Cosgrove and Donal McCartney. *Studies in Irish History*. Dublin: UCD Press, 1979. 150-163.

---. and David Dickson, eds. *The Origins of Popular Literacy in Ireland: Language Change and Educational Development, 1700-1920*. Dublin: Depts. of Modern History, University College Dublin and Trinity College Dublin, 1990.

Dawson, Ciarán. *Peadar Ó Gealacáin: Scríobhaí*. Dublin: Clóchomhar, 1992.

de Brún, Pádraig. *Scriptural Instruction in the Vernacular: the Irish Society and its Teachers, 1818-1827*. Dublin: Institute for Advanced Study, 2009.

de Fréine, Seán. *The Great Silence*. Cork: Mercier, 1978.

de Paor, Liam. *Landscapes with Figures*. Dublin: Four Courts, 1998.

Denvir, Gearóid. "Literature in Irish, 1800-1890, from the Act of Union to the Gaelic League." *The Cambridge History of Irish Literature*. Ed. Margaret Kelleher and Philip O'Leary. Vol. 1. Cambridge: CUP, 2006. 544-598.

Fitzgerald, Garret. *Ireland in the World: Further Reflections*. Dublin: Liberties Press, 2005.

---. "Estimates for Baronies of Minimum Level of Irish Speaking Amongst the Successive Decennial Cohorts, 1771-1781 to 1861-1871." *Proceedings of the Royal Irish Academy* 84C (1984): 117-155.

---. "Irish Speaking in the Pre-Famine Period: A study based on the 1911 census data for people born before 1851 and still alive in 1911." *Proceedings of the Royal Irish Academy* 103C.5 (2003): 5-283.

Fitzpatrick, David. *Irish Emigration 1801-1921*. Dundalk: Irish Economic & Social History Society, 1984.

Gibbons, Luke and Kieran O'Conor, eds. *Charles O'Conor of Ballinagare: Life and Works*. Dublin: Four Courts, 2015.

Hindley, Reg. *The Death of the Irish Language*. Routledge: London, 1990.

Hoban, Brendan. *Turbulent Diocese: the Killala Troubles, 1798-1848*. Dublin: Banley House, 2011.

Hutchinson, John. *The Dynamics of Cultural Nationalism*. London: Allen Unwin, 1987.

Hynes, Eugene. *Knock: The Virgin's Apparition in Nineteenth-Century Ireland*. Cork: Cork UP, 2008.

Kelly, James and Ciarán MacMurchaidh, eds. *Irish and English: Essays on the Irish Linguistic and Cultural Frontier, 1600-1900*. Dublin: Four Courts, 2012.

---. "Introduction: establishing the context." *Irish and English*. 15-42.

Kelly, James and Martyn Powell, eds. *Clubs and Societies in Eighteenth-Century Ireland*. Dublin: Four Courts, 2010.

Larkin, Emmet. "The Devotional Revolution in Ireland, 1850-1875." *American Historical Review* 77.3 (June 1972): 625-52.

Lee, J. J. "On the Accuracy of the pre-Famine Irish Censuses." *Irish Population, Economy and Society*. Ed. J. M. Goldstrom and L. A. Clarkson. Oxford: OUP, 1981. 37-56.

Leerssen, Joep. *Mere Irish and Fíor-Ghael*. Cork: Cork UP, 1996.

---. *Hidden Ireland, Public Sphere*. Galway: Centre for Irish Studies, 2002.

MacDonagh, Oliver. *O'Connell: The life of Daniel O'Connell, 1775-1847*. London: Weidenfeld, 1991.

MacMathúna, Liam. "Verisimilitude or Subversion? Probing the Interaction of English and Irish in Selected Warrants and Macaronic Verse in the Eighteenth Century." Kelly and MacMurchaidh 116-140.

---. *Béarla sa Ghaeilge*. Dublin: Clóchomhar, 2007.

Mac Murchaidh, Ciarán. "The Catholic Church, the Irish Mission and the Irish Language in the Eighteenth Century." Kelly and MacMurchaidh 162-188.

Mahon, William J., ed. *Doctor Kirwin's Irish Catechism*. Cambridge, Mass.: Pangur, 1991.

Máirtín, Caoimhe. *An Máistir*. Dublin: Cois Life, 2003.

McManus, Antonia. *The Irish Hedge School and its Books*, 1695-1831. Dublin: Four Courts, 2002.

Moffett, Miriam. *Soupers and Jumpers: the Protestant Missions in Connemara, 1848-1937*. Dublin: Nonsuch, 2008.

Morley, Vincent, *Ó Chéitinn go Raiftearaí*. Dublin: Coiscéim, 2011.

Murphy, John A. "O'Connell and the Gaelic World." *Daniel O'Connell: Portrait of a Radical*. Ed. Kevin B. Nowlan & Maurice R. O'Connell. Belfast: Appletree, 1984. 32-52.

Murray, Damien. *Romanticism, Nationalism and Irish Antiquarian Societies, 1840-1880* Maynooth: Maynooth UP, 2000.

Ní Mhóráin, Brighid. *Thiar sa Mhainistir atá an Ghaoluinn Bhreá: Meath na Gaeilge in Uíbh Ráthach*. Dingle: An Sagart, 1997.

Ní Mhunghaile, Lisa. "Saothrú Léann na Gaeilge i gCo na Mí san Ochtú agus san Naoú hAois Déag." *Oidhreacht Uí Ghramhnaigh*. Ed. Tracey Ní Mhaonaigh. Maynooth: An Sagart, 2014. 104-128.

Ní Mhurchú, Máire and Diarmuid Breathnach, eds. *Beathaisnéis, 1782–1881*. Dublin: Clóchomhar, 1999.

Nic Pháidín, Caolfhionn and Seán Ó Cearnaigh, eds. *A New View of the Irish Language*. Dublin: Cois Life, 2008.

Ní Úrdail, Meidhbhín. *The Scribe in Eighteenth and Nineteenth-Century Ireland: Motivation and Milieu*. Münster: Nodus, 2000.

Nic Craith, Máiréad. *Malartú Teanga: an Ghaeilge i gCorcaigh san Naoú hAois Déag*. Bremen: Verlag für E.S.I.S. Publikationen, 1994.

Nolan, William, gen. ed. *History and Society*. Dublin: Geography Publications (series).

Ó Buachalla, Breandán. *I mBéal Feirste Cois Cuain*. Dublin: Clóchomhar, 1968.

---. ed. *Cathal Buí: Amhráin*. Dublin: Clóchomhar, 1975.

---. "An Gaodhal' i Meiriceá." *Go Meiriceá Siar*. Ed. Stiofán Ó hAnnracháin. Dublin: Clóchomhar, 1979. 38-56.

---. *Aisling Ghéar*. Dublin: Clóchomhar, 1997.

---. "Canóin na Creille: an File ar Leaba a Bháis." *Nua-Léamha: Gnéithe de Chultúr, Stair agus Polaitíocht na hÉireann, c.1600–c.1900*. Ed. Máirín Ní Dhonnchadha. Dublin: Clóchomhar. 1996. 170-199.

Ó Cadhain, Máirtín. "Conradh na Gaeilge agus an Litríocht." *The Gaelic League Idea*. Ed. Seán Ó Tuama. Cork: Mercier, 1972.

Ó Cadhla, Stiofán. *Civilizing Ireland: Ordnance Survey 1824–1842*. Dublin: Irish Academic Press, 2007.

Ó Chonchúr, Breandán. *Scríobhaithe Chorcaí, 1700–1850*. Dublin: Clóchomhar, 1982.

Ó Ciardha, Éamonn. *Ireland and the Jacobite Cause, 1685–1766: a Fatal Attachment*. Dublin: Four Courts, 2002.

Ó Ciosáin, Niall. *Print and Popular Culture in Ireland, 1750–1850*. Basingstoke: Palgrave, 1997.

---. "Gaelic Culture and Language Shift." *Nineteenth-Century Ireland: a Guide to Recent Research*. Ed. Laurence M. Geary and Margaret Kelleher. Dublin: UCD Press, 2005.

Niall Ó Ciosáin, "Pious miscellanies and spiritual songs: devotional publishing and reading in Irish and Scottish Gaelic, 1760-1900." Kelly and MacMurchaidh 267-282.

Ó Coigligh, Ciarán. *Raifteraí: Amhráin agus Dánta*. Dublin: Clóchomhar, 1987.

Ó Conchúir, Breandán. *Scríobhaithe Chorcaí, 1700–1850*. Dublin: Clóchomhar, 1982.

Ó Cuív, Brian. *Irish Dialects and Irish-Speaking Districts*. Dublin: Institute for Advanced Studies, 1951.

---. "The Irish Language in the Early Modern Period." *A New History of Ireland: Early Modern Ireland 1534-1691*. Ed. T. W. Moody, F. X. Martin and F. J. Byrne. Oxford: OUP, 1976. 509-545.

---. "Irish Language and Literature, 1691-1845." *A New History of Ireland: Eighteenth-Century Ireland*. Ed. W. E. Vaughan & T. W. Moody. Oxford: OUP, 1986. 374-473.

---. "Irish language and literature, 1845-1921." *A New History of Ireland: Ireland under the Union, II: 1870-1921*. Ed. W. E. Vaughan. Oxford: OUP, 1996. 384-435.

Ó Donnchadha, Rónán. *Mícheál Óg Ó Longáin*. Dublin: Coiscéim, 1994.

Ó Drisceoil, Proinsias. *Ar Scaradh Gabhail*. Dublin: Clóchomhar, 2000.

---. "Lámhscríbhinní agus an Léitheoir Coitianta sa 19ú hAois: John O'Daly agus Foinsí *Reliques of Irish Jacobite Poetry*." Ruairí Ó hUiginn, 257-315.

Ó Fiaich, Tomás and Liam Ó Caithnia, eds. *Art Mac Bionaid: Dánta*. Dublin: Clóchomhar, 1979.

Ó Fiannachta, Pádraig. *Léas ar ár Litríocht. Maynooth*: An Sagart, 1974.

---. ed., *Ómós do Eoghan Ó Comhraí*. Dingle: An Sagart, 1995.

Ó Gliasáin, Mícheál, *The Language Question in the Census of Population*. Dublin: ITÉ, 1996.

Ó Gráda, Cormac. *Ireland: A New Economic History, 1780-1939*. Oxford: OUP, 1994.

Ó hÓgáin Dáithí, ed. *Duanaire Osraíoch*. Dublin: Clóchomhar, 1980.

---. ed. *Duanaire Thiobraid Árann*. Dublin: Clóchomhar, 1981.

Ó hUiginn, Ruairí, ed. *Oidhreacht na Lámhscríbhinní: LCC XXXIV*. Maynooth: An Sagart, 2004.

Ó Madagáin, Breandán. *An Ghaeilge i Luimneach, 1700-1900*. Dublin: Clóchomhar, 1974.

Ó Maolmhuaidh, Proinsias. *Uilleog de Búrca: Athair na hAthbheochana*. Dublin: FNT, 1981.

Ó Muraíle, Nollaig. "Seán Ó Donnabháin: An Cúigiú Máistir." *Scoláirí Gaeilge*. Ed. Ruairí Ó hUiginn. Maynooth: An Sagart, 1997. 11-82.

---. "Staid na Gaeilge i gConnachta in aimsir Sheáin Mhic Héil." *Leon an Iarthair*. Ed. Áine Ní Cheannain. Dublin: Clóchomhar, 1983. 37-66.

Ó Murchú, Liam P., ed. *Cinnlae Amhlaoibh Uí Shúilleabháin: Reassessments*. London: Irish Texts Society, 2004.

Ó Murchú, Máirtín. *Cumann Buan-Choimeádta na Gaeilge: Tús an Athréimnithe*. Dublin: Cois Life, 2001.

Ó Néill, Eoghan. *Gleann an Óir*. Dublin: An Clóchomhar, 1988.

Ó Tuathaigh, Gearóid. *Ireland Before the Famine, 1798-1848*. Dublin: Gill and Macmillan, 1972.

Palmer, Patricia. *Language and Conquest in Early Modern Ireland*. Cambridge: CUP, 2001.

Smith, Peter. *Oidhreacht Oirghiall*. Belfast: Ultach Trust, 1995.

Ua Cearnaigh, Barra. *Amhail Fuaim Chogair Bhig*. Dingle: An Sagart, 2011.

Uí Fhlannagáin, Fionnuala. *Mícheál Ó Lócháin agus An Gaodhal*. Dublin: Clóchomhar, 1990.

Wall, Maureen. "The decline of the Irish language" *A View of the Irish Language*. Ed. Brian Ó Cuív. Dublin: Government Publications, 1969.

Whelan, Irene. *The Bible War in Ireland: the "Second Reformation" and the Polarization of Protestant-Catholic Relations, 1800-1840*. Dublin: Lilliput, 2005.

Whelan, Kevin. "The Cultural Effects of the Famine." *The Cambridge Companion to Modern Irish Culture*. Ed. Joe Cleary and Claire Connolly. Cambridge: CUP, 2005. 137-154.

Wolf, Nicholas. "The Irish-Speaking Clergy in the Nineteenth Century: Education, Trends, Timing." *New Hibernia Review* 12.4 (Winter 2008): 68-83.

---. *An Irish-Speaking Island*. Madison: University of Wisconsin Press, 2014.

IMAGES

Cover

Paul Henry, RHA
1876-1958
Cottages, West of Ireland
1928-30
Oil on canvas
22 x 26 in (55.9 x 66 cm)
© 2015 Estate of Paul Henry /
Artists Rights Society (ARS), New
York / IVARO, Dublin
Image provided by Ireland's Great
Hunger Museum, Quinnipiac
University

Figure 1

Detail of Figure 2

Figure 2

Joseph Patrick Haverty
1794-1864
*The Monster Meeting at Clifden
in 1843*
1844
Oil on canvas
43.3 x 72 in (110 x 183 cm)
Photo © National Gallery of Ireland

Figure 3

E. Fitzpatrick
"The Irish School Master"
The Illustrated London News
January 24, 1857
Image provided by National
Library of Ireland

Figure 4

Detail of Figure 3

Figure 5

Engraved by **J. Cochran**
Fl. 1820s – 1860s
John MacHale, Archbishop of Tuam
After an original painting by J.F.
O'Kelly
c. 1820-1870
Image provided by National
Library of Ireland

Figure 6

Cover of *Moore's Melodies,*
translated into Irish by John
McHale
1871

Figure 7

Example of Gaelic script
by scribe **Mícheál Óg Ó Longáin**
(1796)

Figure 8

Frederic William Burton
1816-1900
*Thomas Osborne Davis
(1814-1845), Poet and Politician*
Graphite on paper
7.4 x 4.5 in (18.7 x 11.5 cm)
Photo © National Gallery of
Ireland

Figure 9

Detail of an Irish primer
From *I mBéal Feirste Cois Cuain*
by Breandán Ó Buachalla

Figure 10

James Brenan
News from America
1875
Oil on canvas
32.2 x 35.8 in (82 x 91 cm)
Image provided by Crawford
Art Gallery, Cork

Figure 11

Cover of *An Gaodhal*
April, 1884
Image provided by
National Library of Scotland,
Early Gaelic Book Collection

Figure 12

Cover of *Pious Miscellany*
by Timothy O'Sullivan (Tadhg
Gaelach Ó Súilleabhain)
1829 (10th Edition)

ABOUT THE AUTHOR

Gearóid Ó Tuathaigh is Professor Emeritus in History and formerly Vice-President of the National University of Ireland, Galway. Educated at Galway and at Peterhouse, Cambridge, he has held visiting appointments at universities on both sides of the Atlantic. His academic publications – in Irish and English – relate mainly to modern Irish history and include *Ireland before the Famine 1798-1848*, and he co-edited *Irish Studies: A General Introduction* as well as *Pobal na Gaeltachta: A Scéal agus a Dhán*. He has also published numerous essays on the dynamics of cultural and linguistic change in Ireland from the eighteenth century to the present. A former member of the Senate of the National University of Ireland and of the Ireland-United States Fulbright Commission, Ó Tuathaigh is currently a Member of the Irish Council of State.

IRELAND'S GREAT HUNGER MUSEUM | QUINNIPIAC UNIVERSITY PRESS ©2015

SERIES EDITORS

Niamh O'Sullivan
Grace Brady

IMAGE RESEARCH

Claire Puzarne

DESIGN

Rachel Foley

ACKNOWLEDGMENT

Office of Public Affairs, Quinnipiac University

PUBLISHER

Quinnipiac University Press

PRINTING

GRAPHYCEMS

ISBN 978-0-9904686-7-7

Ireland's Great Hunger Museum
Quinnipiac University

3011 Whitney Avenue
Hamden, CT 06518-1908
203-582-6500

www.ighm.org